MznLnx

Missing Links Exam Preps

Exam Prep for

The Practice of Public Relations

Seitel, 9th Edition

The MznLnx Exam Prep is your link from the texbook and lecture to your exams.
The MznLnx Exam Preps are unauthorized and comprehensive reviews of your textbooks.

All material provided by MznLnx and Rico Publications (c) 2010
Textbook publishers and textbook authors do not particpate in or contribute to these reviews.

MznLnx

Rico Publications

Exam Prep for The Practice of Public Relations
9th Edition
Seitel

Publisher: Raymond Houge
Assistant Editor: Michael Rouger
Text and Cover Designer: Lisa Buckner
Marketing Manager: Sara Swagger
Project Manager, Editorial Production: Jerry Emerson
Art Director: Vernon Lowerui

Product Manager: Dave Mason
Editorial Assitant: Rachel Guzmanji
Pedagogy: Debra Long
Cover Image: Jim Reed/Getty Images
Text and Cover Printer: City Printing, Inc.
Compositor: Media Mix, Inc.

(c) 2010 Rico Publications
ALL RIGHTS RESERVED. No part of this work covered by the copyright may be reproduced or used in any form or by an means--graphic, electronic, or mechanical, including photocopying, recording, taping, Web distribution, information storage, and retrieval systems, or in any other manner--without the written permission of the publisher.

Printed in the United States
ISBN:

For more information about our products, contact us at:
Dave.Mason@RicoPublications.com

For permission to use material from this text or product, submit a request online to:
Dave.Mason@RicoPublications.com

Contents

CHAPTER 1
Defining Public Relations   1

CHAPTER 2
The Growth of Public Relations   7

CHAPTER 3
Communication   9

CHAPTER 4
Management   10

CHAPTER 5
Public Opinion   13

CHAPTER 6
Ethics   15

CHAPTER 7
The Law   18

CHAPTER 8
Research   25

CHAPTER 9
Print Media Relations   30

CHAPTER 10
Electronic Media Relations   34

CHAPTER 11
Employee Relations   36

CHAPTER 12
Multicultural Community Relations   38

CHAPTER 13
Government Relations   40

CHAPTER 14
Consumer Relations   43

CHAPTER 15
Investor Relations   46

CHAPTER 16
International Relations   48

CHAPTER 17
Public Relations Writing   50

CHAPTER 18
Writing for the Eye and Ear   52

CHAPTER 19
Public Relations and the Internet   53

CHAPTER 20
Integrated Marketing Communications   58

Contents (Cont.)

CHAPTER 21
   Crisis Management   64
CHAPTER 22
   The Golden Age   65
ANSWER KEY   67

TO THE STUDENT

COMPREHENSIVE

The *MznLnx* Exam Prep series is designed to help you pass your exams. Editors at MznLnx review your textbooks and then prepare these practice exams to help you master the textbook material. Unlike study guides, workbooks, and practice tests provided by the texbook publisher and textbook authors, *MznLnx* gives you **all** of the material in each chapter in exam form, not just samples, so you can be sure to nail your exam.

MECHANICAL

The MznLnx Exam Prep series creates exams that will help you learn the subject matter as well as test you on your understanding. Each question is designed to help you master the concept. Just working through the exams, you gain an understanding of the subject--its a simple mechanical process that produces success.

INTEGRATED STUDY GUIDE AND REVIEW

MznLnx is not just a set of exams designed to test you, its also a comprehensive review of the subject content. Each exam question is also a review of the concept, making sure that you will get the answer correct without having to go to other sources of material. You learn as you go! Its the easiest way to pass an exam.

HUMOR

Studying can be tedious and dry. MznLnx's instructional design includes moderate humor within the exam questions on occassion, to break the tedium and revitalize the brain

Chapter 1. Defining Public Relations

1. _____ is the practice of managing the flow of information between an organization and its publics. _____ - often referred to as _____ - gains an organization or individual exposure to their audiences using topics of public interest and news items that do not require direct payment. Because _____ places exposure in credible third-party outlets, it offers a third-party legitimacy that advertising does not have.
   a. Symbolic analysis
   b. Power III
   c. Graphic communication
   d. Public Relations

2. _____ LLP, based in Chicago, was once one of the 'Big Five' accounting firms among PricewaterhouseCoopers, Deloitte Touche Tohmatsu, Ernst ' Young and KPMG, providing auditing, tax, and consulting services to large corporations. In 2002, the firm voluntarily surrendered its licenses to practice as Certified Public Accountants in the United States after being found guilty of criminal charges relating to the firm's handling of the auditing of Enron, the energy corporation, resulting in the loss of 85,000 jobs. Although the verdict was subsequently overturned by the Supreme Court of the United States, it has not returned as a viable business.
   a. ACNielsen
   b. AMAX
   c. ADTECH
   d. Arthur Andersen

3. _____ is a term that has been used in various psychology theories, often in slightly different ways (e.g., Goldstein, Maslow, Rogers.) The term was originally introduced by the organismic theorist Kurt Goldstein for the motive to realise all of one's potentialities. In his view, it is the master motive--indeed, the only real motive a person has, all others being merely manifestations of it.
   a. 6-3-5 Brainwriting
   b. 180SearchAssistant
   c. Power III
   d. Self-actualization

4. _____ is a broad label that refers to any individuals or households that use goods and services generated within the economy. The concept of a _____ is used in different contexts, so that the usage and significance of the term may vary.

   A _____ is a person who uses any product or service.

   a. Power III
   b. 180SearchAssistant
   c. 6-3-5 Brainwriting
   d. Consumer

Chapter 1. Defining Public Relations

5. The United States _____ is an independent agency of the United States government created in 1972 through the Consumer Product Safety Act to protect 'against unreasonable risks of injuries associated with consumer products.' As of 2006 its acting chairman is Nancy Nord, a Republican. The other commissioner is Thomas Hill Moore, a Democrat. Normally the board has three commissioners.
   a. 180SearchAssistant
   b. 6-3-5 Brainwriting
   c. Power III
   d. Consumer Product Safety Commission

6. _____ is the deliberate attempt to manage the public's perception of a subject. The subjects of _____ include people (for example, politicians and performing artists), goods and services, organizations of all kinds, and works of art or entertainment.

   From a marketing perspective, _____ is one component of promotion.

   a. Brando
   b. Pearson's chi-square
   c. Little value placed on potential benefits
   d. Publicity

7. _____ is a form of communication that typically attempts to persuade potential customers to purchase or to consume more of a particular brand of product or service. 'While now central to the contemporary global economy and the reproduction of global production networks, it is only quite recently that _____ has been more than a marginal influence on patterns of sales and production. The formation of modern _____ was intimately bound up with the emergence of new forms of monopoly capitalism around the end of the 19th and beginning of the 20th century as one element in corporate strategies to create, organize and where possible control markets, especially for mass produced consumer goods.
   a. ACNielsen
   b. Advertising
   c. AMAX
   d. ADTECH

8. A _____ is a list of the general tasks and responsibilities of a position. Typically, it also includes to whom the position reports, specifications such as the qualifications needed by the person in the job, salary range for the position, etc. A _____ is usually developed by conducting a job analysis, which includes examining the tasks and sequences of tasks necessary to perform the job.

a. 180SearchAssistant
b. Job description
c. 6-3-5 Brainwriting
d. Power III

9. _____ is a strategic management responsibility that integrates finance, communication, marketing and securities law compliance to enable the most effective two-way communication between a company, the financial community, and other constituencies, which ultimately contributes to a company's securities achieving fair valuation. (Adopted by the Ninvestor relationsl Board of Directors, March 2003.) The term describes the department of a company devoted to handling inquiries from shareholders and investors, as well as others who might be interested in a company's stock or financial stability.

a. ADTECH
b. Investor relations
c. AMAX
d. ACNielsen

10. _____ is defined by the American _____ Association as the activity, set of institutions, and processes for creating, communicating, delivering, and exchanging offerings that have value for customers, clients, partners, and society at large. The term developed from the original meaning which referred literally to going to market, as in shopping, or going to a market to sell goods or services.

_____ practice tends to be seen as a creative industry, which includes advertising, distribution and selling.

a. Product naming
b. Customer acquisition management
c. Marketing myopia
d. Marketing

11. _____ refers to messages and related media used to communicate with a market. Those who practice advertising, branding, direct marketing, graphic design, marketing, packaging, promotion, publicity, sponsorship, public relations, sales, sales promotion and online marketing are termed marketing communicators, _____ managers, or more briefly as marcom managers.

a. Marketing communication
b. Merchandise
c. Merchandising
d. Sales promotion

12. _____ is the act of involvement with various media for the purpose of informing the public of an organization's mission, policies and practices in a positive, consistent and credible manner.

Typically, _____ involve coordinating directly with the people responsible for producing the news and features in the mass media. The goal of _____ is to maximize positive coverage in the mass media without paying for it directly through advertising .

a. 6-3-5 Brainwriting
b. 180SearchAssistant
c. Power III
d. Media relations

13. _____ in organizations and public policy is both the organizational process of creating and maintaining a plan; and the psychological process of thinking about the activities required to create a desired goal on some scale. As such, it is a fundamental property of intelligent behavior. This thought process is essential to the creation and refinement of a plan, or integration of it with other plans, that is, it combines forecasting of developments with the preparation of scenarios of how to react to them.
a. 180SearchAssistant
b. 6-3-5 Brainwriting
c. Power III
d. Planning

14. Procter is a surname, and may also refer to:

- Bryan Waller Procter (pseud. Barry Cornwall), English poet
- Goodwin Procter, American law firm
- _____, consumer products multinational

a. Flyer
b. Black PRies
c. Convergent
d. Procter ' Gamble

Chapter 1. Defining Public Relations

15. _____ involves disseminating information about a product, product line, brand, or company. It is one of the four key aspects of the marketing mix. (The other three elements are product marketing, pricing, and distribution). P>_____ is generally sub-divided into two parts:

- Above the line _____: Promotion in the media (e.g. TV, radio, newspapers, Internet and Mobile Phones) in which the advertiser pays an advertising agency to place the ad
- Below the line _____: All other _____. Much of this is intended to be subtle enough for the consumer to be unaware that _____ is taking place. E.g. sponsorship, product placement, endorsements, sales _____, merchandising, direct mail, personal selling, public relations, trade shows

   a. Promotion
   b. Cashmere Agency
   c. Davie Brown Index
   d. Bottling lines

16. _____ is a branch of philosophy which seeks to address questions about morality, such as how a moral outcome can be achieved in a specific situation (applied _____), how moral values should be determined (normative _____), what moral values people actually abide by (descriptive _____), what the fundamental semantic, ontological, and epistemic nature of _____ or morality is (meta-_____), and how moral capacity or moral agency develops and what its nature is (moral psychology.)

Socrates was one of the first Greek philosophers to encourage both scholars and the common citizen to turn their attention from the outside world to the condition of man. In this view, Knowledge having a bearing on human life was placed highest, all other knowledge being secondary.

   a. ACNielsen
   b. ADTECH
   c. AMAX
   d. Ethics

17. An _____ is the manufacturing of a good or service within a category. Although _____ is a broad term for any kind of economic production, in economics and urban planning _____ is a synonym for the secondary sector, which is a type of economic activity involved in the manufacturing of raw materials into goods and products.

There are four key industrial economic sectors: the primary sector, largely raw material extraction industries such as mining and farming; the secondary sector, involving refining, construction, and manufacturing; the tertiary sector, which deals with services (such as law and medicine) and distribution of manufactured goods; and the quaternary sector, a relatively new type of knowledge _____ focusing on technological research, design and development such as computer programming, and biochemistry.

a. AMAX
b. ACNielsen
c. ADTECH
d. Industry

Chapter 2. The Growth of Public Relations

1. Procter is a surname, and may also refer to:

   - Bryan Waller Procter (pseud. Barry Cornwall), English poet
   - Goodwin Procter, American law firm
   - _____, consumer products multinational

   a. Procter ' Gamble
   b. Convergent
   c. Black PRies
   d. Flyer

2. A _____ or digger group is a sociological group that does not constitute a politically dominant voting majority of the total population of a given society. A sociological _____ is not necessarily a numerical _____ -- it may include any group that is subnormal with respect to a dominant group in terms of social status, education, employment, wealth and political power. To avoid confusion, some writers prefer the terms 'subordinate group' and 'dominant group' rather than '_____' and 'majority', respectively.
   a. Reference group
   b. Power III
   c. Minority
   d. Mociology

3. A _____ is an individual who seeks to expose or reveal the real or apparent corruption of businesses or governments to the public. The term originates from members of the Progressive movement in America who wanted to expose the corruption and scandals in government and business. they often wrote about impoverished people and took aim at the established institutions of society.
   a. Muckraker
   b. Shoppers Food ' Pharmacy
   c. Mutual Fund
   d. Predictive validity

4. _____ is the deliberate attempt to manage the public's perception of a subject. The subjects of _____ include people (for example, politicians and performing artists), goods and services, organizations of all kinds, and works of art or entertainment.

   From a marketing perspective, _____ is one component of promotion.

a. Little value placed on potential benefits
b. Brando
c. Pearson's chi-square
d. Publicity

5. _____ is the practice of managing the flow of information between an organization and its publics. _____ - often referred to as _____ - gains an organization or individual exposure to their audiences using topics of public interest and news items that do not require direct payment. Because _____ places exposure in credible third-party outlets, it offers a third-party legitimacy that advertising does not have.
   a. Symbolic analysis
   b. Power III
   c. Graphic communication
   d. Public Relations

6. _____ is a broad label that refers to any individuals or households that use goods and services generated within the economy. The concept of a _____ is used in different contexts, so that the usage and significance of the term may vary.

A _____ is a person who uses any product or service.

   a. Power III
   b. Consumer
   c. 180SearchAssistant
   d. 6-3-5 Brainwriting

7. The _____ is the primary unit in the United States Department of Justice, serving as both a federal criminal investigative body and a domestic intelligence agency. The FBI has investigative jurisdiction over violations of more than 200 categories of federal crime. Its motto is 'Fidelity, Bravery, Integrity,' corresponding to the 'FBI' initialism.
   a. Trademark dilution
   b. Service mark
   c. Federal Bureau of Investigation
   d. Foreign Corrupt Practices Act

Chapter 3. Communication

1. _____ is the practice of managing the flow of information between an organization and its publics. _____ - often referred to as _____ - gains an organization or individual exposure to their audiences using topics of public interest and news items that do not require direct payment. Because _____ places exposure in credible third-party outlets, it offers a third-party legitimacy that advertising does not have.
    a. Graphic communication
    b. Public Relations
    c. Symbolic analysis
    d. Power III

2. _____ describes the situation when output from (or information about the result of) an event or phenomenon in the past will influence the same event/phenomenon in the present or future. When an event is part of a chain of cause-and-effect that forms a circuit or loop, then the event is said to 'feed back' into itself.

    _____ is also a synonym for:

    - _____ Signal; the information about the initial event that is the basis for subsequent modification of the event.
    - _____ Loop; the causal path that leads from the initial generation of the _____ signal to the subsequent modification of the event.

    _____ is a mechanism, process or signal that is looped back to control a system within itself. Such a loop is called a _____ loop.

    a. 6-3-5 Brainwriting
    b. 180SearchAssistant
    c. Feedback
    d. Power III

Chapter 4. Management

1. _____ is the practice of managing the flow of information between an organization and its publics. _____ - often referred to as _____ - gains an organization or individual exposure to their audiences using topics of public interest and news items that do not require direct payment. Because _____ places exposure in credible third-party outlets, it offers a third-party legitimacy that advertising does not have.
    a. Symbolic analysis
    b. Public relations
    c. Power III
    d. Graphic communication

2. _____ in organizations and public policy is both the organizational process of creating and maintaining a plan; and the psychological process of thinking about the activities required to create a desired goal on some scale. As such, it is a fundamental property of intelligent behavior. This thought process is essential to the creation and refinement of a plan, or integration of it with other plans, that is, it combines forecasting of developments with the preparation of scenarios of how to react to them.
    a. Power III
    b. 180SearchAssistant
    c. 6-3-5 Brainwriting
    d. Planning

3. _____ generally refers to a list of all planned expenses and revenues. It is a plan for saving and spending. A _____ is an important concept in microeconomics, which uses a _____ line to illustrate the trade-offs between two or more goods.
    a. 180SearchAssistant
    b. Budget
    c. Power III
    d. 6-3-5 Brainwriting

4. A _____ is a type of bar chart that illustrates a project schedule. A _____ illustrates the start and finish dates of the terminal elements and summary elements of a project. Terminal elements and summary elements comprise the work breakdown structure of the project.
    a. Power III
    b. 6-3-5 Brainwriting
    c. 180SearchAssistant
    d. Gantt chart

5. The Program (or Project) Evaluation and Review Technique, commonly abbreviated _____, is a model for project management designed to analyze and represent the tasks involved in completing a given project.

_____ is a method to analyze the involved tasks in completing a given project, especially the time needed to complete each task, and identifying the minimum time needed to complete the total project.

This model was invented by Booz Allen Hamilton, Inc.

a. Power III
b. 180SearchAssistant
c. 6-3-5 Brainwriting
d. PERT

6. _____ is systematic determination of merit, worth, and significance of something or someone using criteria against a set of standards. _____ often is used to characterize and appraise subjects of interest in a wide range of human enterprises, including the arts, criminal justice, foundations and non-profit organizations, government, health care, and other human services.

Depending on the topic of interest, there are professional groups which look to the quality and rigor of the _____ process.

a. AMAX
b. Evaluation
c. ACNielsen
d. ADTECH

7. The _____, is a model for project management designed to analyze and represent the tasks involved in completing a given project.

_____ is a method to analyze the involved tasks in completing a given project, especially the time needed to complete each task, and identifying the minimum time needed to complete the total project.

PERT was developed primarily to simplify the planning and scheduling of large and complex projects.

a. 6-3-5 Brainwriting
b. Program evaluation and review technique
c. 180SearchAssistant
d. Power III

Chapter 4. Management

8. A _____ is a relatively new executive level position at a corporation, company, organization typically reporting directly to the CEO or board of directors. The _____ is responsible for a brand's image, experience, and promise, and propagating it throughout all aspects of the company. The brand officer oversees marketing, advertising, design, public relations and customer service departments.

   a. Power III
   b. Chief brand officer
   c. Financial analyst
   d. Chief executive officer

9. _____ is a contract between two parties, one being the employer and the other being the employee. An employee may be defined as: 'A person in the service of another under any contract of hire, express or implied, oral or written, where the employer has the power or right to control and direct the employee in the material details of how the work is to be performed.' Black's Law Dictionary page 471 (5th ed. 1979.)

   a. AMAX
   b. ACNielsen
   c. ADTECH
   d. Employment

10. The U.S. _____ is an agency of the United States Department of Health and Human Services and is responsible for regulating and supervising the safety of foods, dietary supplements, drugs, vaccines, biological medical products, blood products, medical devices, radiation-emitting devices, veterinary products, and cosmetics. The FDA also enforces section 361 of the Public Health Service Act and the associated regulations, including sanitation requirements on interstate travel as well as specific rules for control of disease on products ranging from pet turtles to semen donations for assisted reproductive medicine techniques.

    The FDA is an agency within the United States Department of Health and Human Services responsible for protecting and promoting the nation's public health.

    a. 6-3-5 Brainwriting
    b. Food and Drug Administration
    c. 180SearchAssistant
    d. Power III

Chapter 5. Public Opinion

1. _____ is a form of social influence. It is the process of guiding people toward the adoption of an idea, attitude, or action by rational and symbolic (though not always logical) means. It is strategy of problem-solving relying on 'appeals' rather than coercion.
   a. 6-3-5 Brainwriting
   b. Power III
   c. 180SearchAssistant
   d. Persuasion

2. A _____ refers to how a corporation is perceived. It is a generally accepted image of what a company 'stands for'. The creation of a _____ is an exercise in perception management.
   a. Corporate image
   b. Demand generation
   c. Buying center
   d. Lifetime value

3. _____ LLP, based in Chicago, was once one of the 'Big Five' accounting firms among PricewaterhouseCoopers, Deloitte Touche Tohmatsu, Ernst ' Young and KPMG, providing auditing, tax, and consulting services to large corporations. In 2002, the firm voluntarily surrendered its licenses to practice as Certified Public Accountants in the United States after being found guilty of criminal charges relating to the firm's handling of the auditing of Enron, the energy corporation, resulting in the loss of 85,000 jobs. Although the verdict was subsequently overturned by the Supreme Court of the United States, it has not returned as a viable business.
   a. Arthur Andersen
   b. ACNielsen
   c. AMAX
   d. ADTECH

4. _____ is a global document management company which manufactures and sells a range of color and black-and-white printers, multifunction systems, photo copiers, digital production printing presses, and related consulting services and supplies. Xerox is headquartered in Norwalk, Connecticut , though its largest population of employees is based in and around Rochester, New York, the area in which the company was founded. The Xerox 914 was the first one-piece plain paper photocopier, and sold in the thousands.

   Xerox was founded in 1906 in Rochester, New York as 'The Haloid Company', which originally manufactured photographic paper and equipment.

   a. Japan Advertising Photographers' Association
   b. Green Earth Market
   c. Partnership for a Drug-Free America
   d. Xerox Corporation

Chapter 5. Public Opinion

5. The _____ is an English-language international daily newspaper published by Dow Jones ' Company in New York City with Asian and European editions. As of 2007, It has a worldwide daily circulation of more than 2 million, with approximately 931,000 paying online subscribers. It was the largest-circulation newspaper in the United States until November 2003, when it was surpassed by USA Today.
   a. Power III
   b. 180SearchAssistant
   c. 6-3-5 Brainwriting
   d. Wall Street Journal

6. The U.S. _____ is an agency of the United States Department of Health and Human Services and is responsible for regulating and supervising the safety of foods, dietary supplements, drugs, vaccines, biological medical products, blood products, medical devices, radiation-emitting devices, veterinary products, and cosmetics. The FDA also enforces section 361 of the Public Health Service Act and the associated regulations, including sanitation requirements on interstate travel as well as specific rules for control of disease on products ranging from pet turtles to semen donations for assisted reproductive medicine techniques.

The FDA is an agency within the United States Department of Health and Human Services responsible for protecting and promoting the nation's public health.

   a. Power III
   b. Food and Drug Administration
   c. 180SearchAssistant
   d. 6-3-5 Brainwriting

Chapter 6. Ethics 15

1. _____ is a branch of philosophy which seeks to address questions about morality, such as how a moral outcome can be achieved in a specific situation (applied _____), how moral values should be determined (normative _____), what moral values people actually abide by (descriptive _____), what the fundamental semantic, ontological, and epistemic nature of _____ or morality is (meta-_____), and how moral capacity or moral agency develops and what its nature is (moral psychology.)

Socrates was one of the first Greek philosophers to encourage both scholars and the common citizen to turn their attention from the outside world to the condition of man. In this view, Knowledge having a bearing on human life was placed highest, all other knowledge being secondary.

   a. Ethics
   b. ACNielsen
   c. ADTECH
   d. AMAX

2. _____ is the idea that the moral worth of an action is determined solely by its contribution to overall utility: that is, its contribution to happiness or pleasure as summed among all persons. It is thus a form of consequentialism, meaning that the moral worth of an action is determined by its outcome: put simply, the ends justify the means. Utility, the good to be maximized, has been defined by various thinkers as happiness or pleasure (versus suffering or pain), although preference utilitarians like Peter Singer define it as the satisfaction of preferences.
   a. Albert Einstein
   b. African Americans
   c. AStore
   d. Utilitarianism

3. _____ LLP, based in Chicago, was once one of the 'Big Five' accounting firms among PricewaterhouseCoopers, Deloitte Touche Tohmatsu, Ernst ' Young and KPMG, providing auditing, tax, and consulting services to large corporations. In 2002, the firm voluntarily surrendered its licenses to practice as Certified Public Accountants in the United States after being found guilty of criminal charges relating to the firm's handling of the auditing of Enron, the energy corporation, resulting in the loss of 85,000 jobs. Although the verdict was subsequently overturned by the Supreme Court of the United States, it has not returned as a viable business.
   a. ACNielsen
   b. Arthur Andersen
   c. ADTECH
   d. AMAX

4. _____ is the practice of managing the flow of information between an organization and its publics. _____ - often referred to as _____ - gains an organization or individual exposure to their audiences using topics of public interest and news items that do not require direct payment. Because _____ places exposure in credible third-party outlets, it offers a third-party legitimacy that advertising does not have.

Chapter 6. Ethics

   a. Power III
   b. Symbolic analysis
   c. Graphic communication
   d. Public Relations

5. _____ is a form of applied ethics that examines ethical principles and moral or ethical problems that arise in a business environment. It applies to all aspects of business conduct and is relevant to the conduct of individuals and business organizations as a whole. Applied ethics is a field of ethics that deals with ethical questions in many fields such as medical, technical, legal and _____.
   a. 6-3-5 Brainwriting
   b. Business ethics
   c. Power III
   d. 180SearchAssistant

6. The U.S. _____ is an independent agency of the United States government which holds primary responsibility for enforcing the federal securities laws and regulating the securities industry, the nation's stock and options exchanges, and other electronic securities markets. The SEC was created by section 4 of the Securities Exchange Act of 1934 (now codified as 15 U.S.C. Â§ 78d and commonly referred to as the 1934 Act.)
   a. 6-3-5 Brainwriting
   b. Power III
   c. Securities and Exchange Commission
   d. 180SearchAssistant

7. _____ also known as corporate responsibility, corporate citizenship, responsible business, sustainable responsible business and corporate social performance' is a form of corporate self-regulation integrated into a business model. Ideally, _____ policy would function as a built-in, self-regulating mechanism whereby business would monitor and ensure their adherence to law, ethical standards, and international norms. Business would embrace responsibility for the impact of their activities on the environment, consumers, employees, communities, stakeholders and all other members of the public sphere.
   a. Corporate social responsibility
   b. Power III
   c. 180SearchAssistant
   d. 6-3-5 Brainwriting

8. _____ is the pursuit of influencing outcomes -- including public-policy and resource allocation decisions within political, economic, and social systems and institutions -- that directly affect people's current lives. (Cohen, 2001)

Therefore, _____ can be seen as a deliberate process of speaking out on issues of concern in order to exert some influence on behalf of ideas or persons. Based on this definition, Cohen (2001) states that 'ideologues of all persuasions advocate' to bring a change in people's lives.

   a. AMAX
   b. Advocacy
   c. ACNielsen
   d. ADTECH

9. A personal and cultural _____ is a relative ethic _____, an assumption upon which implementation can be extrapolated. A _____ system is a set of consistent _____s and measures that is soo not true. A principle _____ is a foundation upon which other _____s and measures of integrity are based.
   a. Value
   b. Package-on-Package
   c. Supreme Court of the United States
   d. Perceptual maps

Chapter 7. The Law

1. _____ is the deliberate attempt to manage the public's perception of a subject. The subjects of _____ include people (for example, politicians and performing artists), goods and services, organizations of all kinds, and works of art or entertainment.

From a marketing perspective, _____ is one component of promotion.

　a. Little value placed on potential benefits
　b. Brando
　c. Pearson's chi-square
　d. Publicity

2. _____ is a branch of philosophy which seeks to address questions about morality, such as how a moral outcome can be achieved in a specific situation (applied _____), how moral values should be determined (normative _____), what moral values people actually abide by (descriptive _____), what the fundamental semantic, ontological, and epistemic nature of _____ or morality is (meta-_____), and how moral capacity or moral agency develops and what its nature is (moral psychology.)

Socrates was one of the first Greek philosophers to encourage both scholars and the common citizen to turn their attention from the outside world to the condition of man. In this view, Knowledge having a bearing on human life was placed highest, all other knowledge being secondary.

　a. ADTECH
　b. AMAX
　c. ACNielsen
　d. Ethics

3. _____ is the practice of managing the flow of information between an organization and its publics. _____ - often referred to as _____ - gains an organization or individual exposure to their audiences using topics of public interest and news items that do not require direct payment. Because _____ places exposure in credible third-party outlets, it offers a third-party legitimacy that advertising does not have.
　a. Symbolic analysis
　b. Public relations
　c. Power III
　d. Graphic communication

4. The _____ is an English-language international daily newspaper published by Dow Jones ' Company in New York City with Asian and European editions. As of 2007, It has a worldwide daily circulation of more than 2 million, with approximately 931,000 paying online subscribers. It was the largest-circulation newspaper in the United States until November 2003, when it was surpassed by USA Today.

Chapter 7. The Law

   a. 180SearchAssistant
   b. 6-3-5 Brainwriting
   c. Power III
   d. Wall Street Journal

5. _____ is a popular searchable archive of content from newspapers, magazines, legal documents and other printed sources. _____ claims to be the 'world's largest collection of public records, unpublished opinions, forms, legal, news, and business information' while offering their products to a wide range of professionals in the legal, risk management, corporate, government, law enforcement, accounting and academic markets. Typical customers of _____ include lawyers, law students, journalists, and academics.
   a. 180SearchAssistant
   b. 6-3-5 Brainwriting
   c. Power III
   d. LexisNexis

6. _____ in United States law is a condition required to establish libel against public officials or public figures and is defined as 'knowledge that the information was false' or that it was published 'with reckless disregard of whether it was false or not.' Reckless disregard does not encompass mere neglect in following professional standards of fact checking. The publisher must entertain actual doubt as to the statement's truth. This is the definition in only the United States and came from the landmark 1964 lawsuit New York Times Co. v. Sullivan, which ruled that public officials needed to prove _____ in order to recover damages for libel.
   a. Actual malice
   b. ACNielsen
   c. ADTECH
   d. AMAX

7. In law, _____ also called calumny, libel for written words, slander for spoken words, is the communication of a statement that makes a claim, expressly stated or implied to be factual, that may give an individual, business, product, group, government or nation a negative image. It is usually, but not always, a requirement that this claim be false and that the publication is communicated to someone other than the person defamed

In common law jurisdictions, slander refers to a malicious, false and defamatory spoken statement or report, while libel refers to any other form of communication such as written words or images.

   a. Muckraker
   b. Free good
   c. Defamation
   d. Free trade zone

Chapter 7. The Law

8. The U.S. _____ is an independent agency of the United States government which holds primary responsibility for enforcing the federal securities laws and regulating the securities industry, the nation's stock and options exchanges, and other electronic securities markets. The SEC was created by section 4 of the Securities Exchange Act of 1934 (now codified as 15 U.S.C. Â§ 78d and commonly referred to as the 1934 Act.)
   a. 6-3-5 Brainwriting
   b. 180SearchAssistant
   c. Power III
   d. Securities and Exchange Commission

9. _____ is the trading of a corporation's stock or other securities (e.g. bonds or stock options) by individuals with potential access to non-public information about the company. In most countries, trading by corporate insiders such as officers, key employees, directors, and large shareholders may be legal, if this trading is done in a way that does not take advantage of non-public information. However, the term is frequently used to refer to a practice in which an insider or a related party trades based on material non-public information obtained during the performance of the insider's duties at the corporation, or otherwise in breach of a fiduciary duty or other relationship of trust and confidence or where the non-public information was misappropriated from the company.
   a. ACNielsen
   b. ADTECH
   c. Insider trading
   d. AMAX

10. _____ refers to 'controlling human or societal behaviour by rules or restrictions.' _____ can take many forms: legal restrictions promulgated by a government authority, self-_____, social _____, co-_____ and market _____. One can consider _____ as actions of conduct imposing sanctions (such as a fine.) This action of administrative law, or implementing regulatory law, may be contrasted with statutory or case law.
    a. CAN-SPAM
    b. Rule of four
    c. Non-conventional trademark
    d. Regulation

11. _____ is a form of intellectual property which gives the creator of an original work exclusive rights for a certain time period in relation to that work, including its publication, distribution and adaptation; after which time the work is said to enter the public domain. _____ applies to any expressible form of an idea or information that is substantive and discrete. Some jurisdictions also recognize 'moral rights' of the creator of a work, such as the right to be credited for the work.
    a. Celler-Kefauver Act
    b. Reasonable person standard
    c. Collective mark
    d. Copyright

Chapter 7. The Law

12. _____ is the practice of influencing decisions made by government. It includes all attempts to influence legislators and officials, whether by other legislators, constituents or organized groups. A lobbyist is a person who tries to influence legislation on behalf of a special interest or a member of a lobby.

    a. African Americans
    b. AStore
    c. Albert Einstein
    d. Lobbying

13. _____ is a doctrine in United States copyright law that allows limited use of copyrighted material without requiring permission from the rights holders, such as use for scholarship or review. It provides for the legal, non-licensed citation or incorporation of copyrighted material in another author's work under a four-factor balancing test. The term '_____' originated in the United States, but has been added to Israeli law as well; a similar principle, fair dealing, exists in some other common law jurisdictions.

    a. AStore
    b. F. Lee Bailey
    c. African Americans
    d. Fair use

14. _____ is the suppression of speech or deletion of communicative material which may be considered objectionable, harmful, sensitive, or inconvenient to the government or media organizations as determined by a censor.

The rationale for _____ is different for various types of information censored:

- Moral _____, is the removal of materials that are obscene or otherwise morally questionable. Pornography, for example, is often censored under this rationale, especially child pornography, which is censored in most jurisdictions in the world.
- Military _____ is the process of keeping military intelligence and tactics confidential and away from the enemy. This is used to counter espionage, which is the process of gleaning military information. Very often, militaries will also attempt to suppress politically inconvenient information even if that information has no actual intelligence value.
- Political _____ occurs when governments hold back information from their citizens. The logic is to exert control over the populace and prevent free expression that might foment rebellion.
- Religious _____ is the means by which any material objectionable to a certain faith is removed. This often involves a dominant religion forcing limitations on less prevalent ones. Alternatively, one religion may shun the works of another when they believe the content is not appropriate for their faith.
- Corporate _____ is the process by which editors in corporate media outlets intervene to halt the publishing of information that portrays their business or business partners in a negative light.

Strict _____ existed in the Eastern Bloc. Throughout the bloc, the various ministries of culture held a tight reign on their writers. Cultural products there reflected the propaganda needs of the state.

a. Power III
b. 180SearchAssistant
c. 6-3-5 Brainwriting
d. Censorship

15. _____, according to the United States federal law known as the Anticybersquatting Consumer Protection Act, is registering, trafficking in, or using a domain name with bad faith intent to profit from the goodwill of a trademark belonging to someone else. The cybersquatter then offers to sell the domain to the person or company who owns a trademark contained within the name at an inflated price.

The term is derived from 'squatting,' which is the act of occupying an abandoned or unoccupied space or building that the squatter does not own, rent or otherwise have permission to use.

a. Cybersquatting
b. Wildcard DNS record
c. Domain name warehousing
d. Fast flux

16. _____ are legal property rights over creations of the mind, both artistic and commercial, and the corresponding fields of law. Under _____ law, owners are granted certain exclusive rights to a variety of intangible assets, such as musical, literary, and artistic works; ideas, discoveries and inventions; and words, phrases, symbols, and designs. Common types of _____ include copyrights, trademarks, patents, industrial design rights and trade secrets.

a. Elasticity
b. Opinion leadership
c. ACNielsen
d. Intellectual property

17. The _____ of 1990 (ADA) is the short title of United States (Pub.L. 101-336, 104 Stat. 327, enacted July 26, 1990), codified at 42 U.S.C.Â§ 12101 et seq. It was signed into law on July 26, 1990, by President George H. W. Bush, and later amended with changes effective January 1, 2009. The _____ is a wide-ranging civil rights law that prohibits, under certain circumstances, discrimination based on disability. It affords similar protections against discrimination to Americans with disabilities as the Civil Rights Act of 1964,

a. AMAX
b. Americans with Disabilities Act
c. ACNielsen
d. ADTECH

18. The _____, a United States federal law enacted in 1999, is part of A bill to amend the provisions of title 17, United States Code, and the Communications Act of 1934, relating to copyright licensing and carriage of broadcast signals by satellite. It makes people who register domain names that are either trademarks or individual's names with the sole intent of selling the rights of the domain name to the trademark holder or individual for a profit liable to civil action. It was sponsored by Senator Trent Lott on November 17, 1999, and enacted on November 29 of the same year.

a. AMAX
b. ACNielsen
c. ADTECH
d. Anticybersquatting Consumer Protection Act

19. _____ is a broad label that refers to any individuals or households that use goods and services generated within the economy. The concept of a _____ is used in different contexts, so that the usage and significance of the term may vary.

A _____ is a person who uses any product or service.

a. 180SearchAssistant
b. Power III
c. 6-3-5 Brainwriting
d. Consumer

20. _____ is a form of government regulation which protects the interests of consumers. For example, a government may require businesses to disclose detailed information about products--particularly in areas where safety or public health is an issue, such as food. _____ is linked to the idea of consumer rights (that consumers have various rights as consumers), and to the formation of consumer organizations which help consumers make better choices in the marketplace.

a. Trademark dilution
b. Sound trademark
c. Federal Bureau of Investigation
d. Consumer Protection

21. _____s function as professionals who deal with trade, dealing in commodities that they do not produce themselves, in order to produce profit.

_____s can be of two types:

1. A wholesale _____ operates in the chain between producer and retail _____. Some wholesale _____s only organize the movement of goods rather than move the goods themselves.
2. A retail _____ or retailer, sells commodities to consumers (including businesses.) A shop owner is a retail _____.

A _____ class characterizes many pre-modern societies. Its status can range from high (even achieving titles like that of _____ prince or nabob) to low, such as in Chinese culture, due to the soiling capabilities of profiting from 'mere' trade, rather than from the labor of others reflected in agricultural produce, craftsmanship, and tribute.

In the United States, '_____' is defined (under the Uniform Commercial Code) as any person while engaged in a business or profession or a seller who deals regularly in the type of goods sold.

a. Trade credit
b. RFM
c. Merchant
d. Retail loss prevention

22. The _____ was a policy of the United States Federal Communications Commission (FCC) that required the holders of broadcast licenses both to present controversial issues of public importance and to do so in a manner that was (in the Commission's view) honest, equitable and balanced.

The _____ should not be confused with the Equal Time rule. The _____ deals with matters of public importance, while the Equal Time rule deals only with political candidates.

a. Fairness Doctrine
b. 6-3-5 Brainwriting
c. Power III
d. 180SearchAssistant

23. The _____ is an independent agency of the United States government, created, directed, and empowered by Congressional statute , and with the majority of its commissioners appointed by the current President.
a. 180SearchAssistant
b. Federal Communications Commission
c. Power III
d. 6-3-5 Brainwriting

Chapter 8. Research

1. _____ is the practice of managing the flow of information between an organization and its publics. _____ - often referred to as _____ - gains an organization or individual exposure to their audiences using topics of public interest and news items that do not require direct payment. Because _____ places exposure in credible third-party outlets, it offers a third-party legitimacy that advertising does not have.

    a. Power III
    b. Public Relations
    c. Symbolic analysis
    d. Graphic communication

2. _____ is an advertisement in which a particular product specifically mentions a competitor by name for the express purpose of showing why the competitor is inferior to the product naming it.

This should not be confused with parody advertisements, where a fictional product is being advertised for the purpose of poking fun at the particular advertisement, nor should it be confused with the use of a coined brand name for the purpose of comparing the product without actually naming an actual competitor. ('Wikipedia tastes better and is less filling than the Encyclopedia Galactica.')

In the 1980s, during what has been referred to as the cola wars, soft-drink manufacturer Pepsi ran a series of advertisements where people, caught on hidden camera, in a blind taste test, chose Pepsi over rival Coca-Cola.

    a. Comparative advertising
    b. Cost per conversion
    c. GL-70
    d. Heavy-up

3. _____ involves the summary, collation and/or synthesis of existing research rather than primary research, where data is collected from, for example, research subjects or experiments.

The term is widely used in market research and in medical research. The principal methodology in medical _____ is the systematic review, commonly using meta-analytic statistical techniques, although other methods of synthesis, like realist reviews and meta-narrative reviews, have been developed in recent years.

    a. Power III
    b. Secondary research
    c. 6-3-5 Brainwriting
    d. 180SearchAssistant

4. _____ is that part of statistical practice concerned with the selection of individual observations intended to yield some knowledge about a population of concern, especially for the purposes of statistical inference. Each observation measures one or more properties (weight, location, etc.) of an observable entity enumerated to distinguish objects or individuals.

a. Richard Buckminster 'Bucky' Fuller
b. AStore
c. Sports Marketing Group
d. Sampling

5. In statistics, a simple random sample is a subset of individuals (a sample) chosen from a larger set (a population.) Each individual is chosen randomly and entirely by chance, such that each individual has the same probability of being chosen at any stage during the sampling process, and each subset of k individuals has the same probability of being chosen for the sample as any other subset of k individuals (.) This process and technique is known as _____, and should not be confused with Random Sampling.
    a. Logit analysis
    b. Focus group
    c. Market analysis
    d. Simple random sampling

6. _____ is a sampling technique used when 'natural' groupings are evident in a statistical population. It is often used in marketing research. In this technique, the total population is divided into these groups (or clusters) and a sample of the groups is selected.
    a. Cluster sampling
    b. Snowball sampling
    c. Power III
    d. Quota sampling

7. _____ is anything that is intended to save time, energy or frustration. A _____ store at a petrol station, for example, sells items that have nothing to do with gasoline/petrol, but it saves the consumer from having to go to a grocery store. '_____' is a very relative term and its meaning tends to change over time.
    a. Demographic profile
    b. Marketing buzz
    c. MaxDiff
    d. Convenience

8. A _____ is a form of qualitative research in which a group of people are asked about their attitude towards a product, service, concept, advertisement, idea, or packaging. Questions are asked in an interactive group setting where participants are free to talk with other group members.

Ernest Dichter originated the idea of having a 'group therapy' for products and this process is what became known as a _____.

a. Cross tabulation
b. Marketing research process
c. Focus group
d. Logit analysis

9. A _____ is a research instrument consisting of a series of questions and other prompts for the purpose of gathering information from respondents. Although they are often designed for statistical analysis of the responses, this is not always the case. The _____ was invented by Sir Francis Galton.
   a. Questionnaire
   b. Mystery shopping
   c. Mystery shoppers
   d. Market research

10. The general definition of an _____ is an evaluation of a person, organization, system, process, project or product. _____s are performed to ascertain the validity and reliability of information; also to provide an assessment of a system's internal control. The goal of an _____ is to express an opinion on the person/organization/system (etc) in question, under evaluation based on work done on a test basis.
    a. ACNielsen
    b. AMAX
    c. ADTECH
    d. Audit

11. _____ is a broad label that refers to any individuals or households that use goods and services generated within the economy. The concept of a _____ is used in different contexts, so that the usage and significance of the term may vary.

A _____ is a person who uses any product or service.

   a. Consumer
   b. Power III
   c. 6-3-5 Brainwriting
   d. 180SearchAssistant

12. _____ is an American magazine published monthly by Consumers Union. It publishes reviews and comparisons of consumer products and services based on reporting and results from its in-house testing laboratory. It also publishes cleaning and general buying guides.

a. Consumer Reports
b. Power III
c. Crossing the Chasm
d. Magalog

13. _____ is an independent, nonprofit testing and information organization serving consumers in the United States. Its mission is to test products, inform the public, and protect consumers. Its income is derived from the sale of its magazine Consumer Reports and other services, and from noncommercial contributions, grants, and fees.
   a. Checkoff
   b. JPMorgan Chase ' Co.
   c. Goodyear Tire ' Rubber Company
   d. Consumers Union

14. _____ refer to a collection of facts usually collected as the result of experience, observation or experiment or a set of premises. This may consist of numbers, words particularly as measurements or observations of a set of variables. _____ are often viewed as a lowest level of abstraction from which information and knowledge are derived.
   a. Mean
   b. Pearson product-moment correlation coefficient
   c. Data
   d. Sample size

15. _____ is a term used to describe a process of preparing and collecting data - for example as part of a process improvement or similar project.

_____ usually takes place early on in an improvement project, and is often formalised through a _____ Plan which often contains the following activity.

1. Pre collection activity - Agree goals, target data, definitions, methods
2. Collection - _____
3. Present Findings - usually involves some form of sorting analysis and/or presentation.

A formal _____ process is necessary as it ensures that data gathered is both defined and accurate and that subsequent decisions based on arguments embodied in the findings are valid. The process provides both a baseline from which to measure from and in certain cases a target on what to improve. Types of _____ 1-By mail questionnaires 2-By personal interview

- Six sigma
- Sampling (statistics)

a. Power III
b. 6-3-5 Brainwriting
c. Data collection
d. 180SearchAssistant

16. _____ is systematic determination of merit, worth, and significance of something or someone using criteria against a set of standards. _____ often is used to characterize and appraise subjects of interest in a wide range of human enterprises, including the arts, criminal justice, foundations and non-profit organizations, government, health care, and other human services.

Depending on the topic of interest, there are professional groups which look to the quality and rigor of the _____ process.

a. ACNielsen
b. Evaluation
c. ADTECH
d. AMAX

17. _____ is the deliberate attempt to manage the public's perception of a subject. The subjects of _____ include people (for example, politicians and performing artists), goods and services, organizations of all kinds, and works of art or entertainment.

From a marketing perspective, _____ is one component of promotion.

a. Pearson's chi-square
b. Brando
c. Little value placed on potential benefits
d. Publicity

Chapter 9. Print Media Relations

1. _____ is the deliberate attempt to manage the public's perception of a subject. The subjects of _____ include people (for example, politicians and performing artists), goods and services, organizations of all kinds, and works of art or entertainment.

From a marketing perspective, _____ is one component of promotion.

   a. Pearson's chi-square
   b. Brando
   c. Little value placed on potential benefits
   d. Publicity

2. _____ is the act of involvement with various media for the purpose of informing the public of an organization's mission, policies and practices in a positive, consistent and credible manner.

Typically, _____ involve coordinating directly with the people responsible for producing the news and features in the mass media. The goal of _____ is to maximize positive coverage in the mass media without paying for it directly through advertising.

   a. 6-3-5 Brainwriting
   b. 180SearchAssistant
   c. Power III
   d. Media relations

3. _____ is a form of communication that typically attempts to persuade potential customers to purchase or to consume more of a particular brand of product or service. 'While now central to the contemporary global economy and the reproduction of global production networks, it is only quite recently that _____ has been more than a marginal influence on patterns of sales and production. The formation of modern _____ was intimately bound up with the emergence of new forms of monopoly capitalism around the end of the 19th and beginning of the 20th century as one element in corporate strategies to create, organize and where possible control markets, especially for mass produced consumer goods.
   a. ADTECH
   b. AMAX
   c. ACNielsen
   d. Advertising

4. A personal and cultural _____ is a relative ethic _____, an assumption upon which implementation can be extrapolated. A _____ system is a set of consistent _____s and measures that is soo not true. A principle _____ is a foundation upon which other _____s and measures of integrity are based.

Chapter 9. Print Media Relations

31

a. Perceptual maps
b. Supreme Court of the United States
c. Package-on-Package
d. Value

5. A _____ is a relatively new executive level position at a corporation, company, organization typically reporting directly to the CEO or board of directors. The _____ is responsible for a brand's image, experience, and promise, and propagating it throughout all aspects of the company. The brand officer oversees marketing, advertising, design, public relations and customer service departments.

   a. Financial analyst
   b. Power III
   c. Chief brand officer
   d. Chief executive officer

6. The _____ is a very large set of interlinked hypertext documents accessed via the Internet. With a Web browser, one can view Web pages that may contain text, images, videos, and other multimedia and navigate between them using hyperlinks. Using concepts from earlier hypertext systems, the _____ was begun in 1992 by the English physicist Sir Tim Berners-Lee, now the Director of the _____ Consortium, and Robert Cailliau, a Belgian computer scientist, while both were working at CERN in Geneva, Switzerland.

   a. 180SearchAssistant
   b. World Wide Web
   c. Power III
   d. 6-3-5 Brainwriting

7. _____ is an advertisement in which a particular product specifically mentions a competitor by name for the express purpose of showing why the competitor is inferior to the product naming it.

This should not be confused with parody advertisements, where a fictional product is being advertised for the purpose of poking fun at the particular advertisement, nor should it be confused with the use of a coined brand name for the purpose of comparing the product without actually naming an actual competitor. ('Wikipedia tastes better and is less filling than the Encyclopedia Galactica.')

In the 1980s, during what has been referred to as the cola wars, soft-drink manufacturer Pepsi ran a series of advertisements where people, caught on hidden camera, in a blind taste test, chose Pepsi over rival Coca-Cola.

a. GL-70
b. Cost per conversion
c. Heavy-up
d. Comparative advertising

8. _____ is one of the four elements of marketing mix. An organization or set of organizations (go-betweens) involved in the process of making a product or service available for use or consumption by a consumer or business user.

The other three parts of the marketing mix are product, pricing, and promotion.

a. Better Living Through Chemistry
b. Japan Advertising Photographers' Association
c. Comparison-Shopping agent
d. Distribution

9. _____ refer to a collection of facts usually collected as the result of experience, observation or experiment or a set of premises. This may consist of numbers, words particularly as measurements or observations of a set of variables. _____ are often viewed as a lowest level of abstraction from which information and knowledge are derived.

a. Mean
b. Pearson product-moment correlation coefficient
c. Sample size
d. Data

10. _____ is the practice of managing the flow of information between an organization and its publics. _____ - often referred to as _____ - gains an organization or individual exposure to their audiences using topics of public interest and news items that do not require direct payment. Because _____ places exposure in credible third-party outlets, it offers a third-party legitimacy that advertising does not have.

a. Graphic communication
b. Power III
c. Symbolic analysis
d. Public Relations

11. _____ is a methodology in the social sciences for studying the content of communication. Earl Babbie defines it as 'the study of recorded human communications, such as books, websites, paintings and laws.' It is most commonly used by researchers in the social sciences to analyze recorded transcripts of interviews with participants.

_____ is also considered a scholarly methodology in the humanities by which texts are studied as to authorship, authenticity, of meaning.

a. Power III
b. 6-3-5 Brainwriting
c. 180SearchAssistant
d. Content analysis

Chapter 10. Electronic Media Relations

1. A _____ is a video segment created by a PR firm, advertising agency, marketing firm, corporation or government agency and provided to television news stations for the purpose of informing, shaping public opinion commercial products and services.

News reports may incorporate a _____ in whole or part if the news producer feels it contains information appropriate to the story or of interest to viewers.

   a. 180SearchAssistant
   b. 6-3-5 Brainwriting
   c. Power III
   d. Video news release

2. A _____ or community service announcement (CSA) is a non-commercial advertisement broadcast on radio or television, ostensibly for the public interest. _____s are intended to modify public attitudes by raising awareness about specific issues.

The most common topics of _____s are health and safety.

   a. Power III
   b. Public service announcement
   c. 6-3-5 Brainwriting
   d. 180SearchAssistant

3. _____ is an advertisement in which a particular product specifically mentions a competitor by name for the express purpose of showing why the competitor is inferior to the product naming it.

This should not be confused with parody advertisements, where a fictional product is being advertised for the purpose of poking fun at the particular advertisement, nor should it be confused with the use of a coined brand name for the purpose of comparing the product without actually naming an actual competitor. ('Wikipedia tastes better and is less filling than the Encyclopedia Galactica.')

In the 1980s, during what has been referred to as the cola wars, soft-drink manufacturer Pepsi ran a series of advertisements where people, caught on hidden camera, in a blind taste test, chose Pepsi over rival Coca-Cola.

   a. Cost per conversion
   b. GL-70
   c. Comparative advertising
   d. Heavy-up

4. The _____ was a policy of the United States Federal Communications Commission (FCC) that required the holders of broadcast licenses both to present controversial issues of public importance and to do so in a manner that was (in the Commission's view) honest, equitable and balanced.

The _____ should not be confused with the Equal Time rule. The _____ deals with matters of public importance, while the Equal Time rule deals only with political candidates.

　a. Power III
　b. 180SearchAssistant
　c. 6-3-5 Brainwriting
　d. Fairness Doctrine

5. A _____ is the space, actual or metaphorical, in which a market operates. The term is also used in a trademark law context to denote the actual consumer environment, ie. the 'real world' in which products and services are provided and consumed.
　a. Power III
　b. 6-3-5 Brainwriting
　c. 180SearchAssistant
　d. Marketplace

Chapter 11. Employee Relations

1. _____ is a contract between two parties, one being the employer and the other being the employee. An employee may be defined as: 'A person in the service of another under any contract of hire, express or implied, oral or written, where the employer has the power or right to control and direct the employee in the material details of how the work is to be performed.' Black's Law Dictionary page 471 (5th ed. 1979.)
    a. AMAX
    b. ADTECH
    c. Employment
    d. ACNielsen

2. Procter is a surname, and may also refer to:

    - Bryan Waller Procter (pseud. Barry Cornwall), English poet
    - Goodwin Procter, American law firm
    - _____, consumer products multinational

    a. Black PRies
    b. Procter ' Gamble
    c. Convergent
    d. Flyer

3. _____ is the practice of managing the flow of information between an organization and its publics. _____ - often referred to as _____ - gains an organization or individual exposure to their audiences using topics of public interest and news items that do not require direct payment. Because _____ places exposure in credible third-party outlets, it offers a third-party legitimacy that advertising does not have.
    a. Graphic communication
    b. Symbolic analysis
    c. Power III
    d. Public Relations

4. The general definition of an _____ is an evaluation of a person, organization, system, process, project or product. _____s are performed to ascertain the validity and reliability of information; also to provide an assessment of a system's internal control. The goal of an _____ is to express an opinion on the person/organization/system (etc) in question, under evaluation based on work done on a test basis.
    a. ADTECH
    b. ACNielsen
    c. AMAX
    d. Audit

Chapter 11. Employee Relations

5. _____ is an independent technology and market research company that provides its clients with advice about technology's impact on business and consumers. _____ has four research centers in the US: Cambridge, Massachusetts; Foster City, California; Washington, D.C.; and Westport, Connecticut. It also has four European research centers in Amsterdam, Frankfurt, London, and Paris.
   a. BigMachines
   b. Mapinfo
   c. GlobalSpec
   d. Forrester Research

6. _____ is a global document management company which manufactures and sells a range of color and black-and-white printers, multifunction systems, photo copiers, digital production printing presses, and related consulting services and supplies. Xerox is headquartered in Norwalk, Connecticut , though its largest population of employees is based in and around Rochester, New York, the area in which the company was founded. The Xerox 914 was the first one-piece plain paper photocopier, and sold in the thousands.

Xerox was founded in 1906 in Rochester, New York as 'The Haloid Company', which originally manufactured photographic paper and equipment.

   a. Green Earth Market
   b. Partnership for a Drug-Free America
   c. Xerox Corporation
   d. Japan Advertising Photographers' Association

7. _____ is an advertisement in which a particular product specifically mentions a competitor by name for the express purpose of showing why the competitor is inferior to the product naming it.

This should not be confused with parody advertisements, where a fictional product is being advertised for the purpose of poking fun at the particular advertisement, nor should it be confused with the use of a coined brand name for the purpose of comparing the product without actually naming an actual competitor. ('Wikipedia tastes better and is less filling than the Encyclopedia Galactica.')

In the 1980s, during what has been referred to as the cola wars, soft-drink manufacturer Pepsi ran a series of advertisements where people, caught on hidden camera, in a blind taste test, chose Pepsi over rival Coca-Cola.

   a. Heavy-up
   b. Comparative advertising
   c. Cost per conversion
   d. GL-70

Chapter 12. Multicultural Community Relations

1. _____ is a global document management company which manufactures and sells a range of color and black-and-white printers, multifunction systems, photo copiers, digital production printing presses, and related consulting services and supplies. Xerox is headquartered in Norwalk, Connecticut , though its largest population of employees is based in and around Rochester, New York, the area in which the company was founded. The Xerox 914 was the first one-piece plain paper photocopier, and sold in the thousands.

Xerox was founded in 1906 in Rochester, New York as 'The Haloid Company', which originally manufactured photographic paper and equipment.

   a. Japan Advertising Photographers' Association
   b. Xerox Corporation
   c. Partnership for a Drug-Free America
   d. Green Earth Market

2. _____ is the practice of managing the flow of information between an organization and its publics. _____ - often referred to as _____ - gains an organization or individual exposure to their audiences using topics of public interest and news items that do not require direct payment. Because _____ places exposure in credible third-party outlets, it offers a third-party legitimacy that advertising does not have.
   a. Public Relations
   b. Power III
   c. Symbolic analysis
   d. Graphic communication

3. _____ is the pursuit of influencing outcomes -- including public-policy and resource allocation decisions within political, economic, and social systems and institutions -- that directly affect people's current lives. (Cohen, 2001)

Therefore, _____ can be seen as a deliberate process of speaking out on issues of concern in order to exert some influence on behalf of ideas or persons. Based on this definition, Cohen (2001) states that 'ideologues of all persuasions advocate' to bring a change in people's lives.

   a. Advocacy
   b. AMAX
   c. ADTECH
   d. ACNielsen

4. _____ is a rivalry between individuals, groups, nations for territory, a niche, or allocation of resources. It arises whenever two or more parties strive for a goal which cannot be shared. _____ occurs naturally between living organisms which co-exist in the same environment.

a. Price fixing
b. Price competition
c. Competition
d. Non-price competition

5. _____ is the practice of individuals including commercial businesses, governments and institutions, facilitating the sale of their products or services to other companies or organizations that in turn resell them, use them as components in products or services they offer _____ is also called business-to-_____ for short. (Note that while marketing to government entities shares some of the same dynamics of organizational marketing, B2G Marketing is meaningfully different.)
a. Mass marketing
b. Disruptive technology
c. Law of disruption
d. Business marketing

Chapter 13. Government Relations

1. _____ is the practice of managing the flow of information between an organization and its publics. _____ - often referred to as _____ - gains an organization or individual exposure to their audiences using topics of public interest and news items that do not require direct payment. Because _____ places exposure in credible third-party outlets, it offers a third-party legitimacy that advertising does not have.
   a. Symbolic analysis
   b. Power III
   c. Public relations
   d. Graphic communication

2. A _____ is a relatively new executive level position at a corporation, company, organization typically reporting directly to the CEO or board of directors. The _____ is responsible for a brand's image, experience, and promise, and propagating it throughout all aspects of the company. The brand officer oversees marketing, advertising, design, public relations and customer service departments.
   a. Chief executive officer
   b. Chief brand officer
   c. Power III
   d. Financial analyst

3. The _____ is an independent agency of the United States government, established in 1914 by the _____ Act. Its principal mission is the promotion of 'consumer protection' and the elimination and prevention of what regulators perceive to be harmfully 'anti-competitive' business practices, such as coercive monopoly.

The _____ Act was one of President Wilson's major acts against trusts.

   a. Federal Trade Commission
   b. 6-3-5 Brainwriting
   c. Power III
   d. 180SearchAssistant

4. The U.S. _____ is an agency of the United States Department of Health and Human Services and is responsible for regulating and supervising the safety of foods, dietary supplements, drugs, vaccines, biological medical products, blood products, medical devices, radiation-emitting devices, veterinary products, and cosmetics. The FDA also enforces section 361 of the Public Health Service Act and the associated regulations, including sanitation requirements on interstate travel as well as specific rules for control of disease on products ranging from pet turtles to semen donations for assisted reproductive medicine techniques.

The FDA is an agency within the United States Department of Health and Human Services responsible for protecting and promoting the nation's public health.

Chapter 13. Government Relations

a. 180SearchAssistant
b. 6-3-5 Brainwriting
c. Power III
d. Food and Drug Administration

5. The U.S. _____ is an independent agency of the United States government which holds primary responsibility for enforcing the federal securities laws and regulating the securities industry, the nation's stock and options exchanges, and other electronic securities markets. The SEC was created by section 4 of the Securities Exchange Act of 1934 (now codified as 15 U.S.C. § 78d and commonly referred to as the 1934 Act.)
   a. 180SearchAssistant
   b. Power III
   c. 6-3-5 Brainwriting
   d. Securities and Exchange Commission

6. _____ is an advertisement in which a particular product specifically mentions a competitor by name for the express purpose of showing why the competitor is inferior to the product naming it.

This should not be confused with parody advertisements, where a fictional product is being advertised for the purpose of poking fun at the particular advertisement, nor should it be confused with the use of a coined brand name for the purpose of comparing the product without actually naming an actual competitor. ('Wikipedia tastes better and is less filling than the Encyclopedia Galactica.')

In the 1980s, during what has been referred to as the cola wars, soft-drink manufacturer Pepsi ran a series of advertisements where people, caught on hidden camera, in a blind taste test, chose Pepsi over rival Coca-Cola.

   a. Cost per conversion
   b. GL-70
   c. Comparative advertising
   d. Heavy-up

7. The _____ is the primary unit in the United States Department of Justice, serving as both a federal criminal investigative body and a domestic intelligence agency. The FBI has investigative jurisdiction over violations of more than 200 categories of federal crime. Its motto is 'Fidelity, Bravery, Integrity,' corresponding to the 'FBI' initialism.
   a. Foreign Corrupt Practices Act
   b. Federal Bureau of Investigation
   c. Trademark dilution
   d. Service mark

Chapter 13. Government Relations

8. _____ is the practice of influencing decisions made by government. It includes all attempts to influence legislators and officials, whether by other legislators, constituents or organized groups. A lobbyist is a person who tries to influence legislation on behalf of a special interest or a member of a lobby.

   a. Lobbying
   b. African Americans
   c. AStore
   d. Albert Einstein

9. The _____ was legislation aimed at bringing a level of accountability to federal lobbying practices in the United States. The law was amended substantially by the Honest Leadership and Open Government Act of 2007. Under provisions which took effect on January 1, 2006, lobbyists are required to register with the Clerk of the House of Representatives and the Secretary of the Senate.

   a. Scientific controls
   b. BeyondROI
   c. Manufacturers' representatives
   d. Lobbying and Disclosure Act of 1995

10. In the United States, a _____ is the name commonly given to a private group, regardless of size, organized to elect political candidates. Legally, what constitutes a '_____' for purposes of regulation is a matter of state and federal law. Under the Federal Election Campaign Act, an organization becomes a 'political committee' by receiving contributions or making expenditures in excess of $1,000 for the purpose of influencing a federal election.

    a. 6-3-5 Brainwriting
    b. 180SearchAssistant
    c. Political action committee
    d. Power III

Chapter 14. Consumer Relations

1. _____ is a broad label that refers to any individuals or households that use goods and services generated within the economy. The concept of a _____ is used in different contexts, so that the usage and significance of the term may vary.

A _____ is a person who uses any product or service.

   a. 180SearchAssistant
   b. Power III
   c. 6-3-5 Brainwriting
   d. Consumer

2. _____ is an independent, nonprofit testing and information organization serving consumers in the United States. Its mission is to test products, inform the public, and protect consumers. Its income is derived from the sale of its magazine Consumer Reports and other services, and from noncommercial contributions, grants, and fees.

   a. Checkoff
   b. Goodyear Tire ' Rubber Company
   c. JPMorgan Chase ' Co.
   d. Consumers Union

3. The U.S. _____ is an agency of the United States Department of Health and Human Services and is responsible for regulating and supervising the safety of foods, dietary supplements, drugs, vaccines, biological medical products, blood products, medical devices, radiation-emitting devices, veterinary products, and cosmetics. The FDA also enforces section 361 of the Public Health Service Act and the associated regulations, including sanitation requirements on interstate travel as well as specific rules for control of disease on products ranging from pet turtles to semen donations for assisted reproductive medicine techniques.

The FDA is an agency within the United States Department of Health and Human Services responsible for protecting and promoting the nation's public health.

   a. 6-3-5 Brainwriting
   b. 180SearchAssistant
   c. Food and Drug Administration
   d. Power III

4. The _____ is an English-language international daily newspaper published by Dow Jones ' Company in New York City with Asian and European editions. As of 2007, It has a worldwide daily circulation of more than 2 million, with approximately 931,000 paying online subscribers. It was the largest-circulation newspaper in the United States until November 2003, when it was surpassed by USA Today.

a. Power III
b. Wall Street Journal
c. 6-3-5 Brainwriting
d. 180SearchAssistant

5. The United States _____ is an independent agency of the United States government created in 1972 through the Consumer Product Safety Act to protect 'against unreasonable risks of injuries associated with consumer products.' As of 2006 its acting chairman is Nancy Nord, a Republican. The other commissioner is Thomas Hill Moore, a Democrat. Normally the board has three commissioners.
   a. Power III
   b. 6-3-5 Brainwriting
   c. 180SearchAssistant
   d. Consumer Product Safety Commission

6. _____ is an American magazine published monthly by Consumers Union. It publishes reviews and comparisons of consumer products and services based on reporting and results from its in-house testing laboratory. It also publishes cleaning and general buying guides.
   a. Magalog
   b. Power III
   c. Crossing the Chasm
   d. Consumer Reports

7. The _____ is an independent agency of the United States government, established in 1914 by the _____ Act. Its principal mission is the promotion of 'consumer protection' and the elimination and prevention of what regulators perceive to be harmfully 'anti-competitive' business practices, such as coercive monopoly.

The _____ Act was one of President Wilson's major acts against trusts.

   a. 180SearchAssistant
   b. 6-3-5 Brainwriting
   c. Power III
   d. Federal Trade Commission

8. The U.S. _____ is an independent agency of the United States government which holds primary responsibility for enforcing the federal securities laws and regulating the securities industry, the nation's stock and options exchanges, and other electronic securities markets. The SEC was created by section 4 of the Securities Exchange Act of 1934 (now codified as 15 U.S.C. § 78d and commonly referred to as the 1934 Act.)

Chapter 14. Consumer Relations

a. Power III
b. 6-3-5 Brainwriting
c. 180SearchAssistant
d. Securities and Exchange Commission

9. A _____ is a relatively new executive level position at a corporation, company, organization typically reporting directly to the CEO or board of directors. The _____ is responsible for a brand's image, experience, and promise, and propagating it throughout all aspects of the company. The brand officer oversees marketing, advertising, design, public relations and customer service departments.

   a. Financial analyst
   b. Chief executive officer
   c. Power III
   d. Chief brand officer

10. _____ is a form of communication that typically attempts to persuade potential customers to purchase or to consume more of a particular brand of product or service. 'While now central to the contemporary global economy and the reproduction of global production networks, it is only quite recently that _____ has been more than a marginal influence on patterns of sales and production. The formation of modern _____ was intimately bound up with the emergence of new forms of monopoly capitalism around the end of the 19th and beginning of the 20th century as one element in corporate strategies to create, organize and where possible control markets, especially for mass produced consumer goods.

    a. ACNielsen
    b. Advertising
    c. AMAX
    d. ADTECH

Chapter 15. Investor Relations

1. In statistics, _____ has two related meanings:

   - the arithmetic _____
   - the expected value of a random variable, which is also called the population _____.

   It is sometimes stated that the '_____' _____s average. This is incorrect if '_____' is taken in the specific sense of 'arithmetic _____' as there are different types of averages: the _____, median, and mode. For instance, average house prices almost always use the median value for the average. These three types of averages are all measures of locations.

   a. Standard normal distribution
   b. Heteroskedastic
   c. Confidence interval
   d. Mean

2. _____ refers to 'controlling human or societal behaviour by rules or restrictions.' _____ can take many forms: legal restrictions promulgated by a government authority, self-_____, social _____, co-_____ and market _____. One can consider _____ as actions of conduct imposing sanctions (such as a fine.) This action of administrative law, or implementing regulatory law, may be contrasted with statutory or case law.

   a. CAN-SPAM
   b. Non-conventional trademark
   c. Regulation
   d. Rule of four

3. The U.S. _____ is an independent agency of the United States government which holds primary responsibility for enforcing the federal securities laws and regulating the securities industry, the nation's stock and options exchanges, and other electronic securities markets. The SEC was created by section 4 of the Securities Exchange Act of 1934 (now codified as 15 U.S.C. Â§ 78d and commonly referred to as the 1934 Act.)

   a. Power III
   b. 180SearchAssistant
   c. Securities and Exchange Commission
   d. 6-3-5 Brainwriting

4. _____ is a strategic management responsibility that integrates finance, communication, marketing and securities law compliance to enable the most effective two-way communication between a company, the financial community, and other constituencies, which ultimately contributes to a company's securities achieving fair valuation. (Adopted by the Ninvestor relationsl Board of Directors, March 2003.) The term describes the department of a company devoted to handling inquiries from shareholders and investors, as well as others who might be interested in a company's stock or financial stability.

Chapter 15. Investor Relations

a. Investor Relations
b. AMAX
c. ACNielsen
d. ADTECH

Chapter 16. International Relations

1. _____s is the social science that studies the production, distribution, and consumption of goods and services. The term _____s comes from the Ancient Greek οá¼°κονομῖα from οá¼¶κος (oikos, 'house') + vÏŒμος (nomos, 'custom' or 'law'), hence 'rules of the house(hold)'. Current _____ models developed out of the broader field of political economy in the late 19th century, owing to a desire to use an empirical approach more akin to the physical sciences.
    a. ACNielsen
    b. ADTECH
    c. Industrial organization
    d. Economic

2. The _____ is a trilateral trade bloc in North America created by the governments of the United States, Canada, and Mexico. It superseded the Canada-United States Free Trade Agreement between the US and Canada.

Following diplomatic negotiations dating back to 1990 between the three nations, the leaders met in San Antonio, Texas on December 17, 1992 to sign _____.

    a. 180SearchAssistant
    b. 6-3-5 Brainwriting
    c. Power III
    d. North American Free Trade Agreement

3. _____ is the practice of managing the flow of information between an organization and its publics. _____ - often referred to as _____ - gains an organization or individual exposure to their audiences using topics of public interest and news items that do not require direct payment. Because _____ places exposure in credible third-party outlets, it offers a third-party legitimacy that advertising does not have.
    a. Symbolic analysis
    b. Power III
    c. Graphic communication
    d. Public Relations

4. A _____ is a relatively new executive level position at a corporation, company, organization typically reporting directly to the CEO or board of directors. The _____ is responsible for a brand's image, experience, and promise, and propagating it throughout all aspects of the company. The brand officer oversees marketing, advertising, design, public relations and customer service departments.
    a. Power III
    b. Chief executive officer
    c. Financial analyst
    d. Chief brand officer

5. _____ is the practice of individuals including commercial businesses, governments and institutions, facilitating the sale of their products or services to other companies or organizations that in turn resell them, use them as components in products or services they offer _____ is also called business-to-_____ for short. (Note that while marketing to government entities shares some of the same dynamics of organizational marketing, B2G Marketing is meaningfully different.)

a. Mass marketing
b. Disruptive technology
c. Law of disruption
d. Business marketing

6. In grammar, the _____ is the form of an adjective or adverb which denotes the degree or grade by which a person, thing and is used in this context with a subordinating conjunction, such as than, as...as, etc.

The structure of a _____ in English consists normally of the positive form of the adjective or adverb, plus the suffix -er e.g. 'he is taller than his father is', or 'the village is less picturesque than the town nearby'.

a. 6-3-5 Brainwriting
b. Comparative
c. Power III
d. 180SearchAssistant

Chapter 17. Public Relations Writing

1. _____ is the practice of managing the flow of information between an organization and its publics. _____ - often referred to as _____ - gains an organization or individual exposure to their audiences using topics of public interest and news items that do not require direct payment. Because _____ places exposure in credible third-party outlets, it offers a third-party legitimacy that advertising does not have.
   a. Public Relations
   b. Power III
   c. Symbolic analysis
   d. Graphic communication

2. The _____ is an English-language international daily newspaper published by Dow Jones ' Company in New York City with Asian and European editions. As of 2007, It has a worldwide daily circulation of more than 2 million, with approximately 931,000 paying online subscribers. It was the largest-circulation newspaper in the United States until November 2003, when it was surpassed by USA Today.
   a. Power III
   b. 6-3-5 Brainwriting
   c. Wall Street Journal
   d. 180SearchAssistant

3. _____ is a fee paid on borrowed assets. It is the price paid for the use of borrowed money , or, money earned by deposited funds . Assets that are sometimes lent with _____ include money, shares, consumer goods through hire purchase, major assets such as aircraft, and even entire factories in finance lease arrangements.
   a. ACNielsen
   b. AMAX
   c. ADTECH
   d. Interest

4. _____, sometimes called 'news criteria,' determine how much prominence a news story is given by a media outlet, and the attention it is given by the audience. A. Boyd states that: 'News journalism has a broadly agreed set of values, often referred to as 'newsworthinessâ€¦'. _____ are not universal and can vary widely between different cultures. In Western practice, decisions on the selection and prioritization of news are made by editors on the basis of their experience and intuition, although analysis by J. Galtung and M. Ruge showed that several factors are consistently applied across a range of news organizations.
   a. Power III
   b. 6-3-5 Brainwriting
   c. News values
   d. 180SearchAssistant

5. A personal and cultural _____ is a relative ethic _____, an assumption upon which implementation can be extrapolated. A _____ system is a set of consistent _____s and measures that is soo not true. A principle _____ is a foundation upon which other _____s and measures of integrity are based.
   a. Package-on-Package
   b. Perceptual maps
   c. Supreme Court of the United States
   d. Value

Chapter 18. Writing for the Eye and Ear

1. A _____ or community service announcement (CSA) is a non-commercial advertisement broadcast on radio or television, ostensibly for the public interest. _____s are intended to modify public attitudes by raising awareness about specific issues.

The most common topics of _____s are health and safety.

   a. 6-3-5 Brainwriting
   b. Power III
   c. 180SearchAssistant
   d. Public service announcement

2. _____ is an advertisement in which a particular product specifically mentions a competitor by name for the express purpose of showing why the competitor is inferior to the product naming it.

This should not be confused with parody advertisements, where a fictional product is being advertised for the purpose of poking fun at the particular advertisement, nor should it be confused with the use of a coined brand name for the purpose of comparing the product without actually naming an actual competitor. ('Wikipedia tastes better and is less filling than the Encyclopedia Galactica.')

In the 1980s, during what has been referred to as the cola wars, soft-drink manufacturer Pepsi ran a series of advertisements where people, caught on hidden camera, in a blind taste test, chose Pepsi over rival Coca-Cola.

   a. Comparative advertising
   b. GL-70
   c. Cost per conversion
   d. Heavy-up

3. In the United States consumer sales promotions known as _____ or simply sweeps (both single and plural) have become associated with marketing promotions targeted toward both generating enthusiasm and providing incentive reactions among customers by enticing consumers to submit free entries into drawings of chance (and not skill) that are tied to product or service awareness wherein the featured prizes are given away by sponsoring companies. Prizes can vary in value from less than one dollar to more than one million U.S. dollars and can be in the form of cash, cars, homes, electronics, etc.

_____ frequently have eligibility limited by international, national, state, local, or other geographical factors.

   a. Market segment
   b. Claritas Prizm
   c. Commercial planning
   d. Sweepstakes

Chapter 19. Public Relations and the Internet

53

1. _____ is the largest provider of local, long distance telephone services in the United States, and also serves digital subscriber line Internet access. AT'T is the second largest provider of wireless service in the United States, with over 77 million wireless customers, and more than 150 million total customers.

   a. ACNielsen
   b. Intellectual property
   c. AT'T Inc.
   d. Opinion leadership

2. Procter is a surname, and may also refer to:

   - Bryan Waller Procter (pseud. Barry Cornwall), English poet
   - Goodwin Procter, American law firm
   - _____, consumer products multinational

   a. Flyer
   b. Black PRies
   c. Convergent
   d. Procter ' Gamble

3. _____ is a strategic management responsibility that integrates finance, communication, marketing and securities law compliance to enable the most effective two-way communication between a company, the financial community, and other constituencies, which ultimately contributes to a company's securities achieving fair valuation. (Adopted by the Ninvestor relationsl Board of Directors, March 2003.) The term describes the department of a company devoted to handling inquiries from shareholders and investors, as well as others who might be interested in a company's stock or financial stability.

   a. Investor relations
   b. ADTECH
   c. ACNielsen
   d. AMAX

4. _____ is the act of involvement with various media for the purpose of informing the public of an organization's mission, policies and practices in a positive, consistent and credible manner.

Typically, _____ involve coordinating directly with the people responsible for producing the news and features in the mass media. The goal of _____ is to maximize positive coverage in the mass media without paying for it directly through advertising .

a. Power III
b. 6-3-5 Brainwriting
c. 180SearchAssistant
d. Media relations

5. _____ involves disseminating information about a product, product line, brand, or company. It is one of the four key aspects of the marketing mix. (The other three elements are product marketing, pricing, and distribution). P>_____ is generally sub-divided into two parts:

- Above the line _____: Promotion in the media (e.g. TV, radio, newspapers, Internet and Mobile Phones) in which the advertiser pays an advertising agency to place the ad
- Below the line _____: All other _____. Much of this is intended to be subtle enough for the consumer to be unaware that _____ is taking place. E.g. sponsorship, product placement, endorsements, sales _____, merchandising, direct mail, personal selling, public relations, trade shows

a. Cashmere Agency
b. Davie Brown Index
c. Promotion
d. Bottling lines

6. _____ is a popular searchable archive of content from newspapers, magazines, legal documents and other printed sources. _____ claims to be the 'world's largest collection of public records, unpublished opinions, forms, legal, news, and business information' while offering their products to a wide range of professionals in the legal, risk management, corporate, government, law enforcement, accounting and academic markets. Typical customers of _____ include lawyers, law students, journalists, and academics.

a. Power III
b. 180SearchAssistant
c. 6-3-5 Brainwriting
d. LexisNexis

7. The _____ is an English-language international daily newspaper published by Dow Jones ' Company in New York City with Asian and European editions. As of 2007, It has a worldwide daily circulation of more than 2 million, with approximately 931,000 paying online subscribers. It was the largest-circulation newspaper in the United States until November 2003, when it was surpassed by USA Today.

a. 6-3-5 Brainwriting
b. Power III
c. Wall Street Journal
d. 180SearchAssistant

Chapter 19. Public Relations and the Internet

8. _____ is the deliberate attempt to manage the public's perception of a subject. The subjects of _____ include people (for example, politicians and performing artists), goods and services, organizations of all kinds, and works of art or entertainment.

From a marketing perspective, _____ is one component of promotion.

   a. Publicity
   b. Little value placed on potential benefits
   c. Pearson's chi-square
   d. Brando

9. _____ is an advertisement in which a particular product specifically mentions a competitor by name for the express purpose of showing why the competitor is inferior to the product naming it.

This should not be confused with parody advertisements, where a fictional product is being advertised for the purpose of poking fun at the particular advertisement, nor should it be confused with the use of a coined brand name for the purpose of comparing the product without actually naming an actual competitor. ('Wikipedia tastes better and is less filling than the Encyclopedia Galactica.')

In the 1980s, during what has been referred to as the cola wars, soft-drink manufacturer Pepsi ran a series of advertisements where people, caught on hidden camera, in a blind taste test, chose Pepsi over rival Coca-Cola.

   a. Heavy-up
   b. Comparative advertising
   c. Cost per conversion
   d. GL-70

10. An _____ is the manufacturing of a good or service within a category. Although _____ is a broad term for any kind of economic production, in economics and urban planning _____ is a synonym for the secondary sector, which is a type of economic activity involved in the manufacturing of raw materials into goods and products.

There are four key industrial economic sectors: the primary sector, largely raw material extraction industries such as mining and farming; the secondary sector, involving refining, construction, and manufacturing; the tertiary sector, which deals with services (such as law and medicine) and distribution of manufactured goods; and the quaternary sector, a relatively new type of knowledge _____ focusing on technological research, design and development such as computer programming, and biochemistry.

a. Industry
b. ACNielsen
c. AMAX
d. ADTECH

11. A _____ is a professionally managed type of collective investment scheme that pools money from many investors and invests it in stocks, bonds, short-term money market instruments, and/or other securities. The _____ will have a fund manager that trades the pooled money on a regular basis. As of early 2008, the worldwide value of all _____s totals more than $26 trillion.
    a. Mutual Fund
    b. Free trade zone
    c. Promotional mix
    d. Chief marketing officer

12. _____ refers to 'controlling human or societal behaviour by rules or restrictions.' _____ can take many forms: legal restrictions promulgated by a government authority, self-_____, social _____, co-_____ and market _____. One can consider _____ as actions of conduct imposing sanctions (such as a fine.) This action of administrative law, or implementing regulatory law, may be contrasted with statutory or case law.
    a. Rule of four
    b. CAN-SPAM
    c. Regulation
    d. Non-conventional trademark

13. The U.S. _____ is an independent agency of the United States government which holds primary responsibility for enforcing the federal securities laws and regulating the securities industry, the nation's stock and options exchanges, and other electronic securities markets. The SEC was created by section 4 of the Securities Exchange Act of 1934 (now codified as 15 U.S.C. § 78d and commonly referred to as the 1934 Act.)
    a. 6-3-5 Brainwriting
    b. 180SearchAssistant
    c. Power III
    d. Securities and Exchange Commission

14. An _____ is a private network that uses Internet protocols, network connectivity, and possibly the public telecommunication system to securely share part of an organization's information or operations with suppliers, vendors, partners, customers or other businesses. An _____ can be viewed as part of a company's intranet that is extended to users outside the company (e.g.: normally over the Internet.) It has also been described as a 'state of mind' in which the Internet is perceived as a way to do business with a preapproved set of other companies business-to-business (B2B), in isolation from all other Internet users.

Chapter 19. Public Relations and the Internet

a. ADTECH
b. AMAX
c. ACNielsen
d. Extranet

15. _____ is the practice of managing the flow of information between an organization and its publics. _____ - often referred to as _____ - gains an organization or individual exposure to their audiences using topics of public interest and news items that do not require direct payment. Because _____ places exposure in credible third-party outlets, it offers a third-party legitimacy that advertising does not have.
    a. Symbolic analysis
    b. Power III
    c. Graphic communication
    d. Public Relations

16. The term _____ is primarily used by mass media to describe any form of synchronous conferencing, occasionally even asynchronous conferencing. The term can thus mean any technology ranging from real-time online chat over instant messaging and online forums to fully immersive graphical social environments.

Online chat is a way of communicating by sending text messages to people in the same chat-room in real-time.

  a. 6-3-5 Brainwriting
  b. Chat room
  c. Power III
  d. 180SearchAssistant

Chapter 20. Integrated Marketing Communications

1. _____ is the practice of managing the flow of information between an organization and its publics. _____ - often referred to as _____ - gains an organization or individual exposure to their audiences using topics of public interest and news items that do not require direct payment. Because _____ places exposure in credible third-party outlets, it offers a third-party legitimacy that advertising does not have.

   a. Graphic communication
   b. Symbolic analysis
   c. Power III
   d. Public Relations

2. _____ , according to The American Marketing Association, is 'a planning process designed to assure that all brand contacts received by a customer or prospect for a product, service, or organization are relevant to that person and consistent over time.' (Marketing Power Dictionary)

   _____ is a term used to describe a holistic approach to marketing. It aims to ensure consistency of message and the complementary use of media. The concept includes online and offline marketing channels.

   a. ADTECH
   b. AMAX
   c. ACNielsen
   d. Integrated marketing communications

3. _____ is defined by the American _____ Association as the activity, set of institutions, and processes for creating, communicating, delivering, and exchanging offerings that have value for customers, clients, partners, and society at large. The term developed from the original meaning which referred literally to going to market, as in shopping, or going to a market to sell goods or services.

   _____ practice tends to be seen as a creative industry, which includes advertising, distribution and selling.

   a. Customer acquisition management
   b. Product naming
   c. Marketing
   d. Marketing myopia

4. _____ refers to messages and related media used to communicate with a market. Those who practice advertising, branding, direct marketing, graphic design, marketing, packaging, promotion, publicity, sponsorship, public relations, sales, sales promotion and online marketing are termed marketing communicators, _____ managers, or more briefly as marcom managers.

a. Sales promotion
b. Merchandising
c. Marketing communication
d. Merchandise

5. Procter is a surname, and may also refer to:

- Bryan Waller Procter (pseud. Barry Cornwall), English poet
- Goodwin Procter, American law firm
- _____, consumer products multinational

a. Convergent
b. Black PRies
c. Flyer
d. Procter ' Gamble

6. _____ is the deliberate attempt to manage the public's perception of a subject. The subjects of _____ include people (for example, politicians and performing artists), goods and services, organizations of all kinds, and works of art or entertainment.

From a marketing perspective, _____ is one component of promotion.

a. Brando
b. Pearson's chi-square
c. Little value placed on potential benefits
d. Publicity

7. _____ or simply buzz is a term used in word-of-mouth marketing. The interaction of consumers and users of a product or service serve to amplify the original marketing message.

Some describe buzz as a form of hype among consumers, a vague but positive association, excitement, or anticipation about a product or service.

a. Consumption smoothing
b. Consumer confidence
c. Multidimensional scaling
d. Marketing buzz

Chapter 20. Integrated Marketing Communications

8. A _____ is a collection of symbols, experiences and associations connected with a product, a service, a person or any other artifact or entity.

_____s have become increasingly important components of culture and the economy, now being described as 'cultural accessories and personal philosophies'.

Some people distinguish the psychological aspect of a _____ from the experiential aspect.

   a. Brand equity
   b. Brandable software
   c. Store brand
   d. Brand

9. _____ LLP, based in Chicago, was once one of the 'Big Five' accounting firms among PricewaterhouseCoopers, Deloitte Touche Tohmatsu, Ernst ' Young and KPMG, providing auditing, tax, and consulting services to large corporations. In 2002, the firm voluntarily surrendered its licenses to practice as Certified Public Accountants in the United States after being found guilty of criminal charges relating to the firm's handling of the auditing of Enron, the energy corporation, resulting in the loss of 85,000 jobs. Although the verdict was subsequently overturned by the Supreme Court of the United States, it has not returned as a viable business.
   a. ACNielsen
   b. ADTECH
   c. Arthur Andersen
   d. AMAX

10. The term _____, invented to replace the older gender-based terms, is a typical example of a gender-neutral neologism.

In the present media-sensitive world, many organizations are increasingly likely to employ professionals who have received formal training in journalism, communications, public relations and public affairs in this role in order to ensure that public announcements are made in the most appropriate fashion and through the most appropriate channels to maximize the impact of favorable messages, and to minimize the impact of unfavorable messages. Popular local and national sports stars are often chosen as spokespeople for commercial advertising.

   a. Professional services
   b. 180SearchAssistant
   c. Power III
   d. Spokesperson

Chapter 20. Integrated Marketing Communications

11. _____ refers to a type of marketing involving the cooperative efforts of a 'for profit' business and a non-profit organization for mutual benefit. The term is sometimes used more broadly and generally to refer to any type of marketing effort for social and other charitable causes, including in-house marketing efforts by non-profit organizations. Cause marketing differs from corporate giving (philanthropy) as the latter generally involves a specific donation that is tax deductible, while cause marketing is a marketing relationship generally not based on a donation.
    a. Digital marketing
    b. Cause-related marketing
    c. Global marketing
    d. Diversity marketing

12. _____ involves disseminating information about a product, product line, brand, or company. It is one of the four key aspects of the marketing mix. (The other three elements are product marketing, pricing, and distribution). P>_____ is generally sub-divided into two parts:

    - Above the line _____: Promotion in the media (e.g. TV, radio, newspapers, Internet and Mobile Phones) in which the advertiser pays an advertising agency to place the ad
    - Below the line _____: All other _____. Much of this is intended to be subtle enough for the consumer to be unaware that _____ is taking place. E.g. sponsorship, product placement, endorsements, sales _____, merchandising, direct mail, personal selling, public relations, trade shows

    a. Davie Brown Index
    b. Bottling lines
    c. Cashmere Agency
    d. Promotion

13. _____ is a form of communication that typically attempts to persuade potential customers to purchase or to consume more of a particular brand of product or service. 'While now central to the contemporary global economy and the reproduction of global production networks, it is only quite recently that _____ has been more than a marginal influence on patterns of sales and production. The formation of modern _____ was intimately bound up with the emergence of new forms of monopoly capitalism around the end of the 19th and beginning of the 20th century as one element in corporate strategies to create, organize and where possible control markets, especially for mass produced consumer goods.
    a. AMAX
    b. ADTECH
    c. ACNielsen
    d. Advertising

Chapter 20. Integrated Marketing Communications

14. _____ is a global document management company which manufactures and sells a range of color and black-and-white printers, multifunction systems, photo copiers, digital production printing presses, and related consulting services and supplies. Xerox is headquartered in Norwalk, Connecticut , though its largest population of employees is based in and around Rochester, New York, the area in which the company was founded. The Xerox 914 was the first one-piece plain paper photocopier, and sold in the thousands.

Xerox was founded in 1906 in Rochester, New York as 'The Haloid Company', which originally manufactured photographic paper and equipment.

   a. Green Earth Market
   b. Japan Advertising Photographers' Association
   c. Partnership for a Drug-Free America
   d. Xerox Corporation

15. A _____ or digger group is a sociological group that does not constitute a politically dominant voting majority of the total population of a given society. A sociological _____ is not necessarily a numerical _____ -- it may include any group that is subnormal with respect to a dominant group in terms of social status, education, employment, wealth and political power. To avoid confusion, some writers prefer the terms 'subordinate group' and 'dominant group' rather than '_____' and 'majority', respectively.

   a. Reference group
   b. Mociology
   c. Power III
   d. Minority

16. _____ are long-format television commercials, typically five minutes or longer.. _____ are also known as paid programming (or teleshopping in Europe.) Originally, they were a phenomenon that started in the United States where they were typically shown overnight (usually 2:00 a.m. to 6:00 a.m.)
   a. Infomercials
   b. AMAX
   c. ACNielsen
   d. ADTECH

17. _____ is a form of advertisement, where branded goods or services are placed in a context usually devoid of ads, such as movies, the story line of television shows Broadcasting ' Cable reported, 'Two thirds of advertisers employ 'branded entertainment'--_____--with the vast majority of that (80%) in commercial TV programming.' The story, based on a survey by the Association of National Advertisers, added, 'Reasons for using in-show plugs varied from 'stronger emotional connection' to better dovetailing with relevant content, to targetting a specific group.'

_____ became common in the 1980s, but can be traced back to the nineteenth century in publishing.

a. 180SearchAssistant
b. Power III
c. 6-3-5 Brainwriting
d. Product placement

Chapter 21. Crisis Management

1. _____ is the process by which an organization deals with any major unpredictable event that threatens to harm the organization, its stakeholders, or the general public. Three elements are common to most definitions of crisis: (a) a threat to the organization, (b) the element of surprise, and (c) a short decision time.

Whereas risk management involves assessing potential threats and finding the best ways to avoid those threats, _____ involves dealing with the disasters after they have occurred.

   a. Product marketing
   b. Crisis management
   c. Performance measurement
   d. Voice of the customer

2. _____ is a concept that denotes the precise probability of specific eventualities. Technically, the notion of _____ is independent from the notion of value and, as such, eventualities may have both beneficial and adverse consequences. However, in general usage the convention is to focus only on potential negative impact to some characteristic of value that may arise from a future event.
   a. Power III
   b. 180SearchAssistant
   c. 6-3-5 Brainwriting
   d. Risk

3. _____ in organizations and public policy is both the organizational process of creating and maintaining a plan; and the psychological process of thinking about the activities required to create a desired goal on some scale. As such, it is a fundamental property of intelligent behavior. This thought process is essential to the creation and refinement of a plan, or integration of it with other plans, that is, it combines forecasting of developments with the preparation of scenarios of how to react to them.
   a. 180SearchAssistant
   b. 6-3-5 Brainwriting
   c. Power III
   d. Planning

Chapter 22. The Golden Age

1. A _____ is a relatively new executive level position at a corporation, company, organization typically reporting directly to the CEO or board of directors. The _____ is responsible for a brand's image, experience, and promise, and propagating it throughout all aspects of the company. The brand officer oversees marketing, advertising, design, public relations and customer service departments.
    a. Chief executive officer
    b. Financial analyst
    c. Power III
    d. Chief brand officer

2. _____ in its literal sense is the process of transformation of local or regional phenomena into global ones. It can be described as a process by which the people of the world are unified into a single society and function together.

    This process is a combination of economic, technological, sociocultural and political forces.

    a. 180SearchAssistant
    b. Power III
    c. 6-3-5 Brainwriting
    d. Globalization

3. _____ is the practice of managing the flow of information between an organization and its publics. _____ - often referred to as _____ - gains an organization or individual exposure to their audiences using topics of public interest and news items that do not require direct payment. Because _____ places exposure in credible third-party outlets, it offers a third-party legitimacy that advertising does not have.
    a. Graphic communication
    b. Power III
    c. Symbolic analysis
    d. Public Relations

4. _____ was a writer, management consultant, and self-described 'social ecologist.' Widely considered to be the father of 'modern management,' his 39 books and countless scholarly and popular articles explored how humans are organized across all sectors of society--in business, government and the nonprofit world. His writings have predicted many of the major developments of the late twentieth century, including privatization and decentralization; the rise of Japan to economic world power; the decisive importance of marketing; and the emergence of the information society with its necessity of lifelong learning. In 1959, Drucker coined the term 'knowledge worker' and later in his life considered knowledge work productivity to be the next frontier of management.
    a. Paschal Eze
    b. Peter Ferdinand Drucker
    c. Rick Boyce
    d. Nouveau riche

5. _____ is a branch of philosophy which seeks to address questions about morality, such as how a moral outcome can be achieved in a specific situation (applied _____), how moral values should be determined (normative _____), what moral values people actually abide by (descriptive _____), what the fundamental semantic, ontological, and epistemic nature of _____ or morality is (meta-_____), and how moral capacity or moral agency develops and what its nature is (moral psychology.)

Socrates was one of the first Greek philosophers to encourage both scholars and the common citizen to turn their attention from the outside world to the condition of man. In this view, Knowledge having a bearing on human life was placed highest, all other knowledge being secondary.

   a. ADTECH
   b. AMAX
   c. ACNielsen
   d. Ethics

ANSWER KEY

Chapter 1
1. d 2. d 3. d 4. d 5. d 6. d 7. b 8. b 9. b 10. d
11. a 12. d 13. d 14. d 15. a 16. d 17. d

Chapter 2
1. a 2. c 3. a 4. d 5. d 6. b 7. c

Chapter 3
1. b 2. c

Chapter 4
1. b 2. d 3. b 4. d 5. d 6. b 7. b 8. b 9. d 10. b

Chapter 5
1. d 2. a 3. a 4. d 5. d 6. b

Chapter 6
1. a 2. d 3. b 4. d 5. b 6. c 7. a 8. b 9. a

Chapter 7
1. d 2. d 3. b 4. d 5. d 6. a 7. c 8. d 9. c 10. d
11. d 12. d 13. d 14. d 15. a 16. d 17. b 18. d 19. d 20. d
21. c 22. a 23. b

Chapter 8
1. b 2. a 3. b 4. d 5. d 6. a 7. d 8. c 9. a 10. d
11. a 12. a 13. d 14. c 15. c 16. b 17. d

Chapter 9
1. d 2. d 3. d 4. d 5. c 6. b 7. d 8. d 9. d 10. d
11. d

Chapter 10
1. d 2. b 3. c 4. d 5. d

Chapter 11
1. c 2. b 3. d 4. d 5. d 6. c 7. b

Chapter 12
1. b 2. a 3. a 4. c 5. d

Chapter 13
1. c 2. b 3. a 4. d 5. d 6. c 7. b 8. a 9. d 10. c

Chapter 14
1. d   2. d   3. c   4. b   5. d   6. d   7. d   8. d   9. d   10. b

Chapter 15
1. d   2. c   3. c   4. a

Chapter 16
1. d   2. d   3. d   4. d   5. d   6. b

Chapter 17
1. a   2. c   3. d   4. c   5. d

Chapter 18
1. d   2. a   3. d

Chapter 19
1. c   2. d   3. a   4. d   5. c   6. d   7. c   8. a   9. b   10. a
11. a   12. c   13. d   14. d   15. d   16. b

Chapter 20
1. d   2. d   3. c   4. c   5. d   6. d   7. d   8. d   9. c   10. d
11. b   12. d   13. d   14. d   15. d   16. a   17. d

Chapter 21
1. b   2. d   3. d

Chapter 22
1. d   2. d   3. d   4. b   5. d

www.ingramcontent.com/pod-product-compliance
Lightning Source LLC
Chambersburg PA
CBHW081850230426
43669CB00018B/2893